Revivals
in the
Highlands

Revivals
in the
Highlands

by

Angus MacGillivray

REFORMATION PRESS

2016

British Library Cataloguing in Publication Data
ISBN 978-1-872556-20-8
© **Reformation Press 2016**

Published by Reformation Press
11 Churchill Drive, Stornoway
Isle of Lewis, Scotland HS1 2NP

www.reformationpress.co.uk

Also available as a Kindle e-book
(ISBN 978-1-872556-21-5)

Printed by www.lulu.com

Contents

Foreword

In the early eighteenth century a few godly men laboured in the Lord's cause among the many thousands of people who inhabited the wild and remote glens and straths of northern Scotland. The Lord blessed the preaching of these ministers and a great revival of religion began in the counties of Ross and Sutherland. In a relatively short space of time the Lord's right hand wrought wonders of grace in turning many from darkness to light. Truly the desert places rejoiced and blossomed as the rose.

The new converts were favoured with faithful, scriptural preaching from the pulpit and this was supplemented by teaching from local elders and catechists. The people valued the doctrines of grace and became intelligent, exercised and consistent Christians. They were averse to unsound doctrine, formality in religion and lax practice.

Angus MacGillivray was born in 1805 in the mission house at Achness in Strathnaver, Sutherland, where his father, Rev. Duncan MacGillivray, had been ordained as missionary in 1801. In 1817 Duncan MacGillivray became the parish minister of

Lairg. Angus received his formal education at the parish school there and went on to study at the Universities of Aberdeen and Glasgow. He then became schoolmaster at Golspie on the east coast of Sutherland.

In 1828, at the early age of twenty-two, Angus MacGillivray was ordained as minister of the parish of Strathy on the north coast of Sutherland where he laboured faithfully among the scattered congregation. During his university education he had gained some knowledge of medical matters, and he turned this to good account in the parish as the nearest doctor lived many miles away.

In 1841 Angus MacGillivray was translated to the charge of Dairsie in Fife. He left the Church of Scotland at the Disruption in 1843 and continued in Dairsie as the Free Church minister until his death in 1873.

In an era of declension, Angus MacGillivray was a faithful witness for Christ, and an able minister of the New Testament. He ably defended the Sabbath Day in a book of published sermons entitled *The perpetuity of the Sabbath connected with the change of the day.*

An obituary of Rev. Angus MacGillivray was published in the *Monthly Record* of the Free Church of Scotland in 1874. The writer described him as an admirable preacher and stated that his presence brought confidence at a sick or dying bed, for people knew he was no flatterer. The writer also noted that he had a discriminating discernment of cases, he was never satisfied unless the faith of the sick person rested on sufficient Scripture ground, and he was skilful in the application of the Word

During his ministry in Strathy Angus MacGillivray became acquainted with the interesting facts connected with the religion of Easter Ross and Sutherland, which provided the material for the present book, which was originally published in 1859 as *Sketches of Religion and Revivals of Religion in the North Highlands during last Century*. This was one of the first accounts of vital Christianity in the Highlands of Scotland, predating works such as Dr Kennedy's *Days of the Fathers in Ross-shire* (first edition, 1861) and Donald Sage's *Memorabilia Domestica* (1889).

Angus MacGillivray's short book provides a fascinating view of these stirring times. Minor adjustments have been made to the text for clarification and to make the material more attractive to the twenty-first century reader. Footnotes by MacGillivray and the present editor are annotated as [AM] and [RJD] respectively.

In reprinting this book under the title of *Revivals in the Highlands* it is the hope of the publisher that it will stir up present-day readers to fervent prayer that the Lord would visit the present generation with similar showers of blessing. 'Turn us again, O God of hosts, and cause thy face to shine; and we shall be saved' (Psalm 80:7).

The Publisher
Stornoway
June 2016

.

Author's preface

I had the privilege, when very young, of being much in the society of aged ministers and Christians. Their conversation often turned on the state of religion in the North Highlands – what they had seen themselves and what their fathers had told them. Much of what I then heard is of course lost, but much of it still clings to my memory. Now I have often felt that many of these facts might be useful – it would be a pity if all of them should be lost. With the exception of a few short notices in Gillies' *Historical Collections*, nothing, so far as I know, has ever been published on the subject. My main object, therefore, in these pages, is to give a few of the facts somewhat of a permanent record. I have attempted to open what I believe to be a rich mine, and brought out a few pieces of ore. Would that some of my brethren in the north might go on and work it.

Angus MacGillivray, 1859

Introduction

I confine myself in these notices to a particular time and a particular district. The period referred to is the eighteenth century and the beginning of the nineteenth, and the district whose religion during that period I attempt to describe is Easter Ross and the county of Sutherland.

Spiritual religion had existed for ages in that portion of Scotland. It was, in fact, the first part of the Highlands of Scotland which became thoroughly Protestant. And it is interesting to know how the religion of the Bible entered this district and took strong hold of its people, whilst the larger portion of the Highlands was covered with thick darkness.

During the reign of Charles I, three of the great feudal chieftains came in contact with the Truth and felt its power. The Earl of Sutherland, Mackay of Reay and Munro of Foulis were not ashamed of the cross of Christ. The Earl of Sutherland, was the first man to sign the National Covenant in 1638. In 1630 Gustavus Adolphus of Sweden began that struggle in defence of religion which, after his death, gave to the Protestant faith an established footing in Germany. His kingdom being small and his troops at first few in number, he applied for support to the chiefs I have named. These men thoroughly sympathised with him. They saw that the cause was that of religious liberty, and having raised a number of regiments, they sent them to Germany to join the Swedish army. In that army the Scottish soldiers met with real religion, they met with the Bible and learned to read it. Even in a camp they saw God worshipped in spirit and in truth, and many of them were savingly converted. A considerable portion of them fell in battle, but numbers returned to their own country and were the instruments, by the divine blessing, of spreading true religion through their native land. It is interesting, accordingly, to notice that the name Gustavus remained common in that part of Scotland. When the pious soldier returned home and became a father, he called his son after his beloved commander, the Christian king. Thus these districts were Christianised.

In 1678, whilst other parts of the Highlands (Lochaber, for example) were sending 'the Highland Host' to persecute God's people in the Lowlands, the people of Ross and Sutherland were themselves Covenanters, and very many of them were true Christians. Such was the state of things in these districts before the Glorious Revolution of 1688: there was even then living Christianity, and that of a high order. I shall next endeavour to trace the progress of religion after that period, and more particularly during the middle and last part of the eighteenth century.

Chapter 1

Revivals of religion

I shall here notice a few of those extensive awakenings which took place in these districts during the eighteenth century and the start of the nineteenth century.

Nigg

North of Cromarty, where the firth passes between the Sutors, there is a small parish called Nigg. It is almost a peninsula, having one of the Sutors for its extremity at the south.[1]

Some years after the Glorious Revolution, Mr John Balfour became minister of this parish. Tradition still speaks of him as a man of eminent gifts and devoted piety. In 1730, a work of grace began in the parish under the ministry of this man. For some years the work went on very gradually – one here

---

[1] The Sutors of Cromarty are headlands on either side of the entrance to the Cromarty Firth. The North Sutor, near Nigg, rises to 147 metres (486 feet). [RJD]

and one there was brought to know the truth – and there were time after time stops and intermissions. But in 1739 and for years afterwards the awakening became general in the parish. Every day of the week, Saturday not excepted, men and women crowded to the manse, putting the question, 'What must I do to be saved?' They received the gospel and found rest in Christ, and made open profession of their faith, and Mr Balfour remarks that 'not one in forty of those who were awakened had fallen off from a religious profession, or given open scandal to it.' The work was not accompanied with those bodily symptoms which appeared at the same time at Cambuslang and Kilsyth, but the general results proved very clearly that the work was genuine and saving.

Before the awakening the meeting for prayer and conference consisted only of the members of session[2] and a few others, but now two large meetings were held in different districts of the parish, and the body of the people seemed to be under deep, serious impressions. The Lord's Day was observed with the deepest solemnity and (with three or four exceptions) worship was kept up in all the families of the parish. And the outward conduct of the people showed very clearly that this was not mere profession. For many years there was no case

---

[2] The Kirk session consisted of the minister and elders. [RJD]

of crime to be punished by the magistrates, and the Kirk Session had little else to do at their meetings but to confer together as to the state of religion.

Whilst the people were thus 'fervent in spirit, serving the Lord', they were 'not slothful in business'. Most of them were small farmers, and it was remarked at the time that they were 'more forward in the business of their husbandry than their neighbours in other parts of the country'. Many were thus turned from sin unto God, and they continued steadfast in the faith.

Mr Balfour's ministry was eminently blessed, and his name is still remembered with veneration in that part of the country. Old Christians used to speak of a prayer of his which had deeply impressed them. It was the communion Sabbath, and may of God's children had come from distant parishes to receive the Lord's Supper along with their brethren at Nigg. Thousands were assembled at the tent,[3] the tables were in the open air, and Mr Balfour presided. Their communion services in those days were short, but there were so many tables that night was at hand before the last one was finished. The instant it was concluded and a couple of verses sung, Mr Balfour stood up in the tent, and said, 'There is no time for an address – let us pray.' And lifting up his eyes to

---

[3] The tent was a moveable wooden pulpit with a canopy. It was erected in the open air when the congregation was too large for the church at communion seasons. [RJD]

heaven, he said, 'O Lord, we have now done what Thou hast commanded us; do Thou all that Thou hast promised, for the Lord Jesus Christ's sake. Amen.' Then, after praise, he pronounced the benediction and dismissed the immense assembly. Aged Christians were wont to say that they had never heard any prayer which so thrilled their hearts as this brief but comprehensive appeal to God.

The subsequent history of the parish is melancholy. Mr Balfour died, and then a man who had no sympathy with revivals was presented to the parish. The people unanimously protested and, supported by the presbytery, carried their case to the General Assembly. These were the days of high-handed patronage, however. The people lost their case, the man was settled, and the parish of Nigg joined the Secession Church and was lost to the Church of Scotland.

The awakening extended to the neighbouring parishes – to Rosskeen under the ministry of Mr Daniel Bethune, to Kilmuir Easter under that of Mr John Porteous, and to Rosemarkie where Mr John Wood was minister. But instead of dwelling on these cases, let us cross the Dornoch Firth, and see the Lord's work in the county of Sutherland.

Golspie

On a bank overlooking the Moray Firth stands Dunrobin Castle, the seat of the Earls of Sutherland, and on the low ground in the neighbourhood stands the church of Golspie, evidently, from its structure, built in the days of Popery. In the days of Charles II and his brother (James II of England and VII of Scotland), the Sutherland family were the firm supporters of presbyterianism, and many godly persons, driven by persecution from other places, came to Golspie and found shelter there. In 1688 these refugees might have returned to their former homes, 'but such was their gratitude to the family of Sutherland, that they preferred remaining at Golspie under the wings that had covered them in distress'.

Mr Walter Denune was the first minister of Golspie after the Revolution, and though there was no extensive conversion under his ministry, yet at his death in 1730 the parish contained a number of serious Christians.

In 1731 Mr John Sutherland succeeded Mr Denune. He was a man of decided talent, very amiable, and much liked as a man, but the old Christians felt that there was a defect in his preaching – that it lacked something – that it was not, after all, the voice of the Chief Shepherd. But they loved the man and, instead of deserting his ministry, they laid the matter before the Lord. For weeks a few godly men and women met every Saturday in the house of the catechist[4] to pray for their minister and to ask God to give him what they felt he lacked.

One Saturday, having business with the catechist, Mr Sutherland came to the door. Hearing the voice of prayer he stopped to listen, and to his amazement he heard an old venerable man entreating the Hearer of Prayer to give their minister His own Spirit. He left the door without making his presence known, and on Monday he visited the catechist and asked for an explanation. The catechist frankly told him all, and Mr Sutherland said with beautiful simplicity, 'Will you allow me to come to your meeting, and join you in that prayer?' The catechist and his friends cheerfully consented to this. Mr Sutherland joined the meeting, and it was not long till these godly people felt that what was once lacking was now richly supplied.

Mr Sutherland began now to preach with earnestness and unction; he longed for the conversion of his people. For some years, however, there was very little fruit – a few were awakened, but 'their number was so small, and the scandals of others so frequent

---

[4] The catechist was always an elder, and his work was to go from house to house and teach the Shorter Catechism. [AM]

and heinous, that he often concluded his time and labours were almost lost.'

In these circumstances, having been at the General Assembly, he visited Kilsyth and Cambuslang and Muthil. On his return home he told his people what he had seen and heard, and he persuaded the few serious people to hold meetings for prayer in the different districts of the parish. And now at last there was a manifest shaking among the bones. There was little outward manifestation; the only thing visible at first was 'a decent, grave, and solemn deportment, and shedding abundance of tears'. The people were, in fact, so anxious to conceal their feelings that, as Mr Sutherland quaintly expressed it, he had to shew them doctrinally that it is the duty of the awakened not only to tell their case to the Saviour, but also to ministers and experienced Christians. But though the work advanced quietly, it advanced steadily, and the result was that in less than nine months from the very beginning of it, seventy persons in that small country parish came to their minister with the question, 'What must we do to be saved?' And this was no mere temporary impression: the work went on for years. It extended to the neighbouring parish of Rogart and the result was a large number of solid, enlightened Christian people, in whose daily walk the image of Christ was seen – 'living epistles of Christ, known and read of all men'.

21

Strathnaver

In the north of Sutherland there is a magnificent strath, thirty miles long. Passing up from the ocean, you wind along by the side of a noble river, its banks richly clothed with the native birch, till you reach Loch Naver, from which it flows. At the upper end of the loch, rising up almost perpendicularly, as if presiding over the scene and protecting it, stands Ben Klibreck, more than 3000 feet high.

Strathnaver is part of the parish of Farr, and in 1727 Mr Andrew Robertson was settled as minister of that parish. The parish church stood at the foot of the strath and, as the population of the whole parish must have exceeded three thousand in those days, Mr Robertson's work was a very arduous one. But his heart was in the work; he laboured in season and out of season, and there was a general awakening of souls extending over the parish.

When matters were in this state, the people of Kiltearn in Ross-shire gave Mr Robertson a call. The case came before the church courts and, though the Earl of Sutherland appeared at the bar of the Assembly resisting the translation, the Assembly were so impressed with the importance of Kiltearn (once the parish of Mr Thomas Hogg) that Mr Robertson was translated.

The people of Farr felt this to be a fearful trial, and they felt it all the more that Mr Robertson's successor was not a man of the same spirit. The feeling of the people is brought out by a simple anecdote. A few years after the translation, some godly people from Farr went across the country to attend a communion in Ross-shire. Mr Robertson was one of the assistants, and on Monday he preached one of his rich gospel sermons at the tent. During the sermon one of the Farr men became much excited and, at last, began sobbing aloud. Some fellow Christian, disturbed by the man's sobs, turned to him and entreated him to be silent. His answer was, 'How can I be silent, how can I but sob, when I see the precious food that was rightfully mine richly dispensed to others, whilst my own soul is starving at home?'

But even during this 'Moderate' incumbency, which did not last long, God did not forget His people or His work in Strathnaver. In 1745, the Jacobite rebellion broke out and Mr Porteous of Kilmuir, being threatened by the rebels, took refuge in a glen which lies at the head of the strath and at the base of the mountain. He lived there for months, preaching the gospel of peace as few could preach it, and during that short period his labours were manifestly blessed in turning sinners to God.

At last the Moderate minister was removed and Mr George Munro was settled, and was for many years minister of Farr. He was a man very eminent for piety and zeal and boldness.

I have seen the eyes of old Christians kindle when they spoke of him, and the fruits of his ministry were great and permanent. He had a special love for Strathnaver, and mainly through his efforts a church was built in the strath, about the middle of the eighteenth century, and the Committee for the Royal Bounty provided it with a minister.

I shall have occasion to refer to Strathnaver in a future page, but I may here record the testimony of my late venerated father who began his ministry among this people. In his old age, he said, 'I was well acquainted with the Highlands of Scotland, and I knew the state of religion in the Highlands, in Inverness-shire, Ross-shire and Sutherland. But as regards the number of decidedly converted people or the character of their religion, I never knew any place where the religion of Christ so shone and flourished and pervaded the community as it did in Strathnaver.'

Tongue

North and west of Strathnaver is the parish of Tongue. Its church and manse lie on the bank of a beautiful arm of the sea. Ben Loyal, with its rugged peaks, looks down on them at the distance of five miles. The parish contains the mansion house of what was once the Reay family – a family noted, in days gone by, for its piety and its kindness to the poor.

Mr William Mackenzie was the minister of Tongue for sixty-five years. After being missionary at Strathnaver for three years, he was settled at Tongue on the call of the people in 1769. He found them disposed to be kind to himself personally, but he found them also careless and ignorant and worldly.

For four years after his induction his preaching produced no impression. Carelessness seemed to increase and he began to lose heart. On the Lord's Day the practice was to have three services consecutively – first Gaelic, then English, and then Gaelic again, all without an interval. When the few English-speaking people retired, the young people, who of course understood nothing but Gaelic, left the church instead of remaining for the afternoon Gaelic service. This distressed him and he was anxious to know what these people did when they deserted the afternoon service. Once a Christian friend came to visit and Mr Mackenzie asked him to slip out along with the young people and to observe them. His friend's report was that they stood in the churchyard and indulged in all manner of worldly conversation and frivolity, and on that very day a horse had been sold and bought.

The minister's mind was deeply wounded, almost overwhelmed, and he resolved to make his feelings known. Next Lord's Day, therefore, when the usual rush took place, he addressed them in a voice of authority, and requested all who had Gaelic to resume their seats as he had something to say to them. All of them obeyed at once. They were, for the moment, awed, and amid breathless silence he addressed them as follows. 'I came to this parish four years ago, on your unanimous call, and I had then the impression that I had God's call too. But I fear I have been mistaken. I am doing no good among you; the gospel is making no impression on you. What is worse, you are hardening under it. Instead of receiving it, you flee from it, and leave God's house on His own day to buy and sell in the churchyard. I trust the Lord will remove me to some other place where I shall not be utterly useless, as I am here. "Woe is me, that I sojourn in Mesech, that I dwell in the tents of Kedar!"' And then he burst into tears and sat down in the pulpit, and for the next five minutes wept and sobbed – his feelings were too strong for utterance. Having at last mastered his feelings, he rose to preach, and with a power and a pathos which were peculiar to himself, he proclaimed to his people the unsearchable riches of Christ.

It was the day of the Lord's visitation, the turning point in the history of that people. From that day forward there was a blessed outpouring of the Spirit of God. He told me himself (and he was a man incapable of vain boasting) that for years afterwards he never preached on the Lord's Day but some of his people during the ensuing week – at times as many as six or eight – came to him under the conviction of sin, asking the way to Jesus.

I knew Mr Mackenzie intimately, and I remember asking him what were the truths in his preaching which seemed to have been specially blessed for producing this awakening. And I never could forget his answer. As I well knew, he was not one who harped on one string. He was a comprehensive divine, deeply read in the English and Dutch theology, but he told me that the truth which seemed to impress and awaken his people above all others was the dying love of Christ. It was the sin of despising and rejecting this love that made them restless and wretched and self-condemned, till they found the appointed remedy in the love itself.

Through the blessing of the Spirit the work was an extensive and permanent one, and what he had found a desolate wilderness became as the garden of the Lord.

Chapter 2

General results

Having thus sketched a few cases of general awakening, I shall now describe the effects produced on the religion of the North Highlands and the character of the people. And I do this the more especially because I have found much misapprehension prevailing in the Lowlands in regard to this subject.

The men

Many have heard of 'the men' of the north. A common impression in regard to them is that they were a set of troublesome persons, who were always thorns in the sides of the ministers, seeking to lord it over them, and that their religion was a dark, uncomfortable system, wholly subjective, which led them always to look to themselves and their feelings instead of looking to Christ in the Word. Let me notice these misapprehensions, for misapprehensions they most certainly are.

It is quite true that the godly men of the north had no faith in mere ordination – they were not Puseyites.[5] If a man was manifestly careless and worldly and graceless, and if his preaching was not the preaching of the cross, they did not regard him as a minister of Christ at all. If a man of this stamp was settled in the parish where they lived, they would not sit under his ministry; they believed that in so doing they put their souls in peril, and rather than do it they walked their ten or twelve miles on a Sabbath morning to the church of the nearest evangelical minister. As a boy I have seen the very backs of the seats crowded with such hearers. But if they believed that the man was really sent by Christ and that his heart was in the work – let him be never so young, never so inexperienced, never so much filled with trembling at the responsibilities of his office – these men, the oldest and most godly among them, loved him, prayed for him, looked up to him and encouraged his heart in the Lord. And his own people not only looked up to him as *a* minister but as *their* minister. He would be a bold man that would dare in their presence to speak disrespectfully of him.

---

[5] Followers of Edward Pusey and his associates in the Oxford Movement (Tractarians) within the Church of England. The 'High Church' views they adopted included the error of apostolic succession. The Puseyites became Anglo-Catholics and many joined the Roman Catholic Church. [RJD]

Let me give an example of the relation in which minister and people stood to one another. A young minister was settled in a district which contained a large number of enlightened Christians, and they received him warmly from the first as a minister of Christ. After he had been a few years with them his soul got into deep waters. Satan was suffered to assail the foundations of his faith and for some months he had not a ray of comforting light. He was a reserved man and concealed his feelings, and continued to preach amid deep mental suffering.

On a Sabbath afternoon, whilst concluding the service with prayer, intense misery extorted the following petition: 'Lord, have pity on those of Thy servants who endeavour to declare to others the comforts of the Gospel, whilst they cannot themselves taste a single drop.' In the evening the catechist, an old venerable Christian man, noted for his deep, enlightened piety, called at the manse. He put the question, 'What did you mean by that petition in your prayer?' And when the minister sought to evade the question, he said with the deepest tenderness, 'I know your state of mind. I have been in the same state. Tell me all.' Thus encouraged, the minister told him candidly the state of mind he had been in for months past. The old man listened till his minister was done and then, from a full heart, he spoke for half an hour of the glory of Christ – his unsearchable love and the fulness and freeness of his salvation – and how he himself had got deliverance in similar trials. And before he ceased, the minister's bonds were loosed and God restored to him the joy of his salvation. And can anyone suppose that such dealings with their minister would breed presumption among these men? No, the very reverse would be the case! Next Lord's Day that old man would sit, like a little child, listening to the gospel proclaimed by his young minister.

This was a fair specimen of the *real* men of the north. The sketch is not a fancied one: the thing was told me with deep feeling by the minister himself – my own father – and I have myself met with many of these men who showed the very same spirit. There was in them a beautiful combination of faithfulness and tenderness.

In April 1843, having gone to Sutherland and met one of these men, we happened to speak of a minister in that country. After a flaming profession of evangelism and of zeal for certain church principles, the minister had flung the whole overboard. On my remarking that it was a melancholy case of apostasy, his answer was 'Yes, but I was prepared for it. God is very jealous of His glory and I saw what was coming. I happened to be at a sacrament where he assisted, and I saw foolish people offering incense to him. That, however, might have been, without affecting his character. But I saw him *receiving* the worship, and I felt that man must have a fall.' Happening to add, 'You are, sir, the second person to whom I ever mentioned this,' I enquired who the first person was. And then he told me with some reluctance, 'Well, sir, I spoke to the man himself at the time. I thought it my duty to tell him the thing and to warn him. But till now I never mentioned it to another human being.'

It is true they were keen-sighted. They abhorred hypocrisy, and when they detected the *affectation* of piety, they gave it no quarter. A student of theology called for one of them, and apparently unable to give utterance to his feeling, he kept weeping for a time. The old man asked him why he wept, and he replied, 'I am looking forward to the ministry and I am overwhelmed with the fear that I have not God's call.' I knew the old man well – he was full of the milk of human kindness – but he had deep discernment and he saw at a glance through the weeper and he answered solemnly, 'My advice to you is, take good heed that you don't enter the ministry till you get God's call.' The old man was right. The student went on and became a minister and was afterwards deposed for gross immorality.

But whilst the men were thus discerning and not easily imposed on, they had very much of the tenderness of Christ, and where the discovered honesty and earnestness and real anxiety, they encouraged enquirers and took the deepest interest in their welfare. I have known one of them, when eighty years of age, spend nights in prayer for a young minister whom he knew to be at the time in a state of darkness and discouragement.

In a word, then, the real men of the north, instead of despising the ministry, were its strength and support.

Religion in the North Highlands

As to the character of their religion it is quite true that they pressed very strongly the necessity of conversion. They held all religion to be worthless that did not reconcile the heart to God's character and law, and so general was this feeling that the most careless believed *in a certain sense* that unless they were converted by the Spirit they could not be saved – and not only so, but true believers held very strongly that the only evidence of being in a state of salvation was the work of the Spirit in the soul and the fruits of the Spirit in the life. But then they never dreamed of putting the work of the Spirit in place of the work of Christ, or in putting Christ in the heart in the place of Christ in the Word. A common saying, which was often on their lips, brings this out: 'The awakened sinner says, if I were holy I would come to Christ; Christ says, come to me, a sinner as thou art, and I will make thee holy.'

When I look back on the sermons I have heard and my conversations with venerable Christian people, I can without hesitation say that their religion was at the least as thoroughly *objective* as anything I have since come in contact with. The glorious person of Christ, God manifest in the flesh, free justification through His imputed righteousness; the fulness of the Spirit in Christ for the purpose of quickening dead souls and sanctifying the members of His body; the free access which sinners as such have to Christ; His gracious invitation to every sinner to come to Him *now*, and His promise to be at once the reconciled God of all that come to Him, and all this connected with man's total depravity and God's electing love – such were the doctrines which the ministers preached and the people of the north believed. It is a mistake, therefore, to suppose (as some have done) that they made religion to consist in doubting their own salvation.

It is true they had their seasons of darkness and doubt and temptation, and you would meet one here and there who, like Mr Fearing in the *Pilgrim's Progress* was all his days pressed down with the fear of coming short, whilst all who knew him saw the image of Christ in him. I have known such, and I have seen that, like Mr Fearing, when they came to the river, all was light and peace. All this is true, for the men were in earnest; their religion was not that of 'children playing in the market place'. But take them as a whole, I never knew more cheerful Christians or persons who seemed to enjoy so much of the light of God's countenance. And some of them could speak of divine manifestations, such as we meet with in the diary of Jonathan Edwards.

Their religion was thoroughly the reverse of what was dark and gloomy. Let me give an example or two. An old man past sixty, who had spent his days in carelessness and worldliness, was at that age brought to know Christ. From the day of his conversion, he gave himself wholly to the things of eternity and enjoyed peace in believing. He came at last to die, and he then enjoyed the full assurance of hope. One of his sons, a godly man, said to him with all tenderness, 'Would it not be right in you, who lived so long without God in the world, carefully to scrutinise the foundation of that strong hope?' The old man started up in bed and said, 'Don't trouble me with your doubts. I know Him whom I trust. The grip which He took of me and which I took of Him, when I was hanging over hell, He will never let go and I will never let go through all eternity.'

Take another example. An old man of eighty was for the first time confined to bed whilst the sacrament of the Supper was dispensed in his own parish. I knew him well, and I cannot help naming him, for I owe him much. His name was Angus Gunn, the worthy catechist of Lairg, my father's parish. Calling for him one evening during the communion, I found his mind exercised with these words: 'Come with me, my love, from Lebanon.' He happened to remark that Lebanon was the mountain of delights, and on my asking what he meant, he spoke as follows. 'I have been deeply exercised all this day. It is not any doubt I have of my interest in Christ; God has made that very clear to me – it were ungrateful to deny it. But I have been putting the question, why am I confined to this bed on the communion week, whilst my brethren have gone up to the mountain of ordinances? I could call God to witness that I took delight in His ordinances, and these words impressed me as if they said, "Come with *me*, my love, from the mountain of delights. You must now learn the lesson to live on Christ alone without public ordinances."'

I could give numerous examples of the same kind, and they would all show that the religion of these men was eminently objective, that it was the religion of direct faith in Christ.

It is quite true that one acquainted with the north could point to individuals of a different stamp. There were latterly, in *certain districts*, persons who took pleasure in railing against ministers, persons in whom pride and censoriousness were but too apparent and whose religion, so far as one could judge, was that of persons whose consciences had at one time been awakened and who had felt the terrors of the Lord, but who had never found rest in Christ.

I have met with some of them and their religion, so far as I could see, was altogether subjective, for it seemed to have no connection with the cross of Christ. They seemed to me to have at the first grasped at peace and comfort – not as lost sinners believing Christ's free call and coming to Him as sinners, but as persons who believed themselves to be the elect of God, and such a faith necessarily produced anything but the fruits of humility and love. But the true men of the north shunned their fellowship and denounced them, and they were but a very small portion compared with the solid, enlightened Christians.

I have read descriptions of 'the men' of the north in which these sectaries had evidently sat for the picture and I have been indignant at the gross injustice of the thing. It was just as unfair as if, in describing the Puritans in England in the days of the Commonwealth, the Ranters and Fifth Monarchy men described by Baxter were given as a specimen of the whole class. The truth is, wherever there is real religion we are sure to have Satan's counterfeit, and though these sectaries sometimes annoyed us, we could not get rid of them. In the Lowlands there were half a score of sects, some one of which would absorb these restless spirits; in the north we had no dissent, and our sectaries professed to be members of the Church of Scotland.

A Christian community

Let me glance for a little at the effect produced on general society by this state of religious feeling and character. And to make the thing more graphic I shall take a single district, one already referred to: Strathnaver.

The land was in the hands of middlemen, under what was called the *wadset* system,[6] a system now abolished, and the resident gentlemen were practically the proprietors and drew the rents. They were educated men, many of whom had been in the army and had seen the world. The general population occupied farms under them, and whilst these farms were large enough to support their families and to give them full employment during most of the year, they had still time for reading and reflection.

In each township or hamlet you would find two or three able, godly men, to whom all looked up. The influence of these men over all classes was very great. In their presence iniquity hid its face. It was not the influence of fear; it was that of character – of strict integrity and meekness and love. Even such of the gentlemen as were not themselves, perhaps,

---

[6] A mortgage of land given by a borrower to a lender. [RJD]

under the power of religion, regarded these men with feelings of strong respect.

I may illustrate this by a somewhat amusing anecdote. A wicked, litigious person prosecuted one of the leading Christians, and the case was tried before the resident justices. After examining witnesses, the Court found that there was not a particle of evidence, and that the charge was unjust and vexatious. When decreet (formal judgment) was given, the disappointed litigant, addressing the magistrates, said, 'Well, though I have not got justice here, there is a court above you that will do me justice.' The presiding magistrate was a retired military officer and a very able man. Turning to the man, he asked, 'Do you mean to appeal to the Quarter-sessions?'[7] and the answer was 'No. I appeal to the Judge of all.' The magistrate's instant reply was, 'Poor blockhead, I knew you to be a knave, but I never till now thought you a fool. For whatever chance you might have against Gordon in a court composed of poor sinners like me, you have no chance whatever against him in *that* court.' The magistrate was not one who made a profession of religion, but he could recognise and appreciate in Gordon the beauty of the Christian character.

---

[7] The quarterly court of the justices of the peace of a particular county. [RJD]

And to see the state of society among these people, let us look at them on the Lord's Day. It is the Sabbath morning and they are preparing to go to the house of God. They are up early, for many of them are seven or eight miles from the church. After breakfast and family worship, they are ready to start. At last the leading Christian men leave their houses. All the rest assemble around them and, a portion of Scripture being named, religious conversation begins. The younger people are silent, but they listen with deep interest whilst one venerable man after another speaks from a full heart about the love of Christ to perishing sinners and the work of the Spirit in the soul. When half-way to church, they sit down to rest and, after singing a few verses to one of their pleasant airs, prayer is offered up for the outpouring of the Spirit and for a blessing on the Word they are to hear, and for Christ's presence with His servant who is about to speak in His name. At last the several groups unite, and eight hundred people assemble in the house of God, very many of them hungering for the bread of life, looking to God to feed their souls.

When the service is over, the several groups return, each to their own hamlet, and after taking the necessary food, they meet in the house of one of the leading men. He begins with prayer and praise. He then makes the people repeat all they remember of the sermons they have heard, throwing in practical remarks of his own, and pressing the reception of the Truth. And after a portion of the Catechism has been repeated and the service closed with prayer, the people retire to their own homes to worship God in the family.

Such was Strathnaver in 1800, sixty years ago – what is it now? The beautiful strath, once occupied by sixteen hundred people, contains now some thousands of sheep and some thirty families, consisting mostly of shepherds – excellent people, but not one of them a native of the strath. Political economy will call this improvement, for the change brings to our markets more sheep and wool. I enter not into this question – I have nothing to do with it. All I shall say is that the change has destroyed and scattered to the winds of heaven as noble an example of a Christian community as Scotland ever beheld. The roofless walls of the church are still there, surrounded by the graves of these old worthies, but the people are gone, never to return.

Chapter 3

Illustrative sketches

Let me still further illustrate the subject by drawing – I do not say portraits, but a few sketches of individuals, two of them private Christians and two of them ministers. And though they all, in a sense, belonged to the eighteenth century, they lived to such an age that I myself had the privilege of knowing them. And my object here is not so much to do honour to these individuals as to show how different their religion was from the repulsive picture that has sometimes been drawn of North Highland religion.

Mr Hugh Mackenzie

Mr Hugh Mackenzie was born in Kilmuir Easter, in 1728, and when he was a very young man he was brought to know the Truth. After enjoying for a time the peace and rest of the gospel, he was assailed with dark temptations, tending to infidelity and atheism. Having gone to his minister, Mr Porteous, and told him of this, he received the following rather singular answer: 'Ah, are you assailed with these dreadful temptations? I had thought that Satan reserved these for us ministers. You must look to God Himself; man can do nothing for you. One comfort, however, I can give you. Whilst these temptations continue, you are in no danger of becoming careless – *the wheels of your soul will gather no rust.*'

After a severe struggle, he was not only delivered from these temptations, but a foundation was laid for that strong, childlike faith which was, all his life, the most striking feature in his character.

At the age of twenty-five, he was advanced to the eldership, and, some years after, he left Ross-shire and came to reside in Sutherland. He there enjoyed the ministry of the late godly Mr Rainy, father of Dr Rainy of Glasgow University.[8] On Mr Rainy's death, a Moderate minister was settled in Creich at the point of the bayonet, and the whole population, with Hugh Mackenzie at their head, deserted the parish church. They did not, however, leave the Church of Scotland. When the weather permitted, they went to neighbouring parishes to hear the gospel, and when this could not be, Hugh Mackenzie, who was now near eighty, assembled the people on the Lord's Day at a well-known 'rock' in the parish. There he and others engaged in devotional exercises and read the Scriptures and evangelical sermons, frequently those of Boston. This, of course, excited the wrath

---

[8] Dr Harry Rainy was Professor of Forensic Medicine. He was the father of Dr Robert Rainy, the notorious liberal leader in the Free Church during the latter part of the nineteenth century. [RJD]

of the parish minister, and for some years no other minister was permitted to admit Mr Mackenzie to the Lord's Supper.

Having two sons in the ministry, he went to reside with one of them, and there I met him for the first time. I was at once struck with his cheerfulness and the marvellous confidence he had in God. It is this that has led me to refer to him specially, and I must give some examples of it.

An eminent minister, who had often met him, was struck with his habitual assurance. And in order that he might know the foundation of it, he went to visit him, a distance of thirty miles. To draw him out, he said to him, 'Mr Mackenzie, you are a man to be envied. You know nothing of doubts and fears; you always enjoy the full assurance of hope.' The old man replied at once, 'Yes, yes, I understand you. Many a man speaks of my strong faith who does not know all it has to struggle with. But I shall tell you what my faith is. I am the emptiest, vilest, poorest sinner I know on the face of the earth. I feel myself to be so. But I read in His own Word that He heareth the cry of the poor, and I believe Him, and I cry to Him and He always hears me. And that is all the faith or assurance I have got.' The venerable minister, on telling me the incident, made the remark: 'If I know anything of true faith, Mr Mackenzie's faith is a most scriptural and a most rational one.'

Some years before his death I happened to be at his son's house when the Lord's Supper was dispensed in the parish. On Monday Mr Mackenzie went to the tent to hear an old minister with whom he had been long intimate, and the text was 'He will speak peace to his people, and to his saints.' The wind happened to be high and, when the sermon was over, the minister said to him, 'I fear, Mr Mackenzie, you were not hearing well.' 'Yes,' was the answer. 'I was hearing all day, and believing too.' In the evening I accompanied his sons to call for the old man. When the question was put, 'How do you feel tonight?' his answer was, 'My case is more easily felt than described. You read that there is a peace of God which passeth all understanding, and a joy unspeakable, and full of glory, and that is just my case tonight.' When further questioned, he remarked, 'I got into this state of mind whilst hearing that precious sermon today.' And then, addressing his sons, he said, 'Don't think that I despise your preaching. You preach the gospel, and I bless God for it, but you have not the experience of the old minister. The preaching we had today about the peace is what suits my soul.'

In 1829 he began to sink and his son was sent for. On being asked by his son what his views were now as to the things of eternity, he answered with beautiful simplicity, 'I leave it all in His own hands. I am not able to think much, but I know He won't send me to hell.' When his end was evidently near, and when asked how he felt, he was able to whisper, 'He has been entertaining me with a promise,' and soon after he breathed his last in the one hundred and first year of his age.

Jane Mackay

Jane Mackay lived at Armadale, in what is now the parish of Strathy. The death of her first husband, when she was very young, was the means of awakening her, and after a severe conflict she was brought to know the Saviour.

When I became acquainted with her, she was an old woman and I a very young minister, and being a member of my congregation I had many dealings with her. One of the first things which struck me was a simple incident, which showed her exquisite tenderness. Calling for her on Monday, I found her seriously ill and I discovered that she had got ill in church the previous day in consequence of the crowd and the heat. And on my asking, 'Why did you not at once go out?' her answer was, 'My dear, had you been an older minister, I would have gone out. But foolish people might have said that I left the church because I disliked something in the sermon, and I thought it a far higher duty to remain in the church, sick as I was, than do what might in the very least injure your usefulness or even hurt your feelings.' She was indeed tender-hearted.

With a strong, masculine understanding her heart was one of the warmest I ever knew. I never knew a Christian in whom the warmth of youthful impressions and the solidity of one long exercised to godliness were so combined – and combined to the last. At eighty years of age, if you read to her the account of the crucifixion or her favourite chapter, the fifty-third of Isaiah, the big tears instantly ran down her face, showing the love that was felt within. Christ was to her a living, present person, who was always with her, and with whom she held the closest fellowship.

And yet her religion was eminently practical. A young woman, one of my people, who was under deep convictions of sin, called for her. The young woman was married and had a family. After drawing her out, Jane at last said to her, 'I hope you are active in looking after your household.' The poor woman replied, 'I am in that state of mind I can attend to nothing.' Upon which Jane said, 'That will never do. Don't expect to get peace while you are neglecting duty. I have often been on a harvest day in a state of deep mental suffering, yet there was not a woman on the harvest field who cut down more corn than I did. I felt that whatever came of me, I must not give the world occasion to dishonour Christ by saying that my religion made me idle and thriftless.'

Her confidence in God was that of the little child. She had passed through very severe afflictions, and in describing these to me, she said, 'You have heard of my last trial. My two lovely sons both drowned in one night – their bodies are still in the Pentland Firth.' On my remarking that that must have been a fearful trial, she said, 'Yes, greatly more fearful than my neighbours had any thought of. I felt it duty to conceal my feelings and to make my sufferings known only to my gracious Father. And yet I had my consolations too. The first time I crossed the hill and saw the Pentland Firth, where my sons were lost, I began to weep bitterly, and to rebel against the providence of God. And then, as if the voice had come from heaven, I heard Him say to me, 'I gave My Son for thee, and thou grudgest thy sons to Me.' The effect was perfect: I was brought in a moment to cheerful submission. I exclaimed with joy, "O Lord, not my will, but Thine, be done!"'

I almost never knew anyone who seemed so much to make God's will her rule in everything. One evening she sent for me, and on my arrival I found her dangerously ill and suffering excruciating pain. In those days, being more than twenty miles from the nearest medical aid, I had to prescribe for my people and to supply them with medicine. And though in this case I dreaded the worst, I resolved to make the trial. I brought her the medicine in a cup, and when I asked her to take it, she at once refused. Her words were, 'I am more than eighty years of age. During all that time I have never taken medicine of any kind, and I really cannot take it.' I reasoned with her, but she was firm. At last I remembered there was an argument which was almost sure to prevail. I said, 'Jane, what is required in the sixth commandment? You know the sixth commandment requireth all lawful endeavours to preserve *our own* life as well as the life of others.' The effect was instantaneous. She said immediately, 'I did not think of that. His will is precious; there must be no disobedience to it. Give me the cup!' After holding it in her hands for more than two minutes, evidently engaged in prayer, she turned round to see that there was none in the room but myself, and then she said with a smile, 'I shall tell you something which I would not tell everyone, but it may do you good and help to encourage you. It is very likely that this is my last night on earth, and that I am just entering the eternal world. But what you have put into that cup gives me more terror than all the innumerable sins of a long life, for I know that they are all blotted out in the blood of the Lamb.' She recovered from that illness, however, and lived for years after, her Christian graces shining forth more brightly than ever.

She had an intense thirst for the salvation of her fellow-creatures. In her own meek, cheerful, engaging way, she sought to win to Christ all who came in contact with her. A young lady, who was on a visit in the parish, called to take leave of her before returning home. The old woman had been completely bedridden for some years. When about to take leave, the young girl said, 'I shall soon be back and see you again.' Jane's reply was, 'No, my dear. Don't expect to see me again. It's just sinful to wish that my life should be prolonged. I long to be home, and above all, bedridden as I am, I am utterly useless.' The lady replied, 'Nonsense. You are not useless! How do you know but that beautiful, cheerful religion of yours may be the means of alluring and drawing to Christ young persons like me?' The old woman started up in her bed, her eyes kindled, and she said with deep feeling, 'My dear, if I thought that by remaining here I could be the instrument of bringing a single soul to Christ, I'd cheerfully lie here till I withered.'

When disabled from active work she spent much of her time in intercessory prayer. On telling me that she could never sleep at night – that any sleep she got was during the day – I remarked that she must find the night very long. Her answer was, 'No. I often find it too short. I spend it in prayer for my friends. I begin with my own family. I then leave home and I pay you a visit when you are probably sleeping, and I always visit Mr Munro at Halkirk. I then go to Edinburgh and Glasgow and I next cross the Atlantic, for I have Christian friends in America.

And before I get through all my friends, the night has passed and the daylight is come.'

I cannot describe the circumstances of her death. When I left that country she was still spared. But I have the full assurance that her end was peace and that she is now before the throne.

Rev. William Mackenzie

We have already seen Mr Mackenzie as the earnest and successful minister. He was the brother of Mr Hugh Mackenzie, and was born in Ross-shire in 1738. I may add that the two Mackenzies who died at Tongue in 1845 were his son and grandson.

He was in early life brought to know the Truth. Having gone to Inverness at the time of the communion, Mr James Calder of Croy preached on Sabbath from the words 'Look to me and be ye saved, all the ends of the earth' and this sermon was the means of drawing him to Christ. He then resolved to devote himself to the ministry. Being an earnest student and enjoying the acquaintance and friendship of such men as Fraser of Alness, Porteous of Kilmuir and MacPhail of Resolis, he became a workman that needeth not to be ashamed. And during his ministry he continued to be a laborious student. He told me that for many years he had made it a rule to have all his sermons written out, and his English sermon committed on Friday evening at the latest.

When I went to the presbytery of which he was a member, he was ninety-two years of age and quite blind. And yet even then he was about the most fascinating companion I ever met. There was a freshness and a heartiness and a joyfulness about him, such as I never saw in so old a man. It was partly natural temperament, but it was also spiritual attainment. Bunyan would have said of him (and said truly) that he had got to the land of Beulah, within sight of the city.

He had a special love for young men and for young ministers, and seemed to enjoy their society more than that of older men. He delighted in instructing and encouraging young people, placing religion before them in its more attractive aspects and cheerfully giving them the results of his own observation and experience. But still he knew his own position; no-one could take improper liberties with him. He at once put down presumption. And when in his latter days he came in contact with the censorious system I have alluded to, he gave it no quarter – he never hesitated in denouncing it as the work of Satan.

To the very last he took delight in preaching. I have seen him when he was ninety-three go to a tent and preach vigorously, making himself heard by at least a thousand people, and at this time he was quite blind, so that I had to read the chapter and the psalms for him.

It was by preaching that he brought on the illness from which he died. The parish was a large one, and his son had gone to preach in a district at a distance from the church. The people in the neighbourhood of the church had assembled as usual to hold a prayer meeting with the elders. The old minister was by that time unable to leave the manse; and having heard that there was no preaching in the church, he said to his daughter-in-law, 'Send for these people. Let them come to the manse and I shall preach to them.' The people came to the manse, filling the lower rooms and the lobby and the staircase, and then the venerable man preached in Gaelic and English, raising his voice so as to be heard by all. But the effort was too much. He was ninety-six years of age. Slight inflammation of the lungs came on, and nature would not rally so as to throw it off.

Hearing of his last illness, I lost no time in coming to visit him. Finding him in bed, and alluding to his illness, I said, 'I fear you have not been taking care of yourself – preaching was too much for you.' He replied, 'I did not think it right that the people should be without preaching when I was so near and able to address them.' Upon this, I said, 'Ah sir, your heart was in the work.' He got excited and said,

'Yes, my heart is in the work – there is nothing on earth I care for but the work. I know that Christ sent me to the work, I know that He gave me success in the work, and I know that when I get to heaven, many a soul from the parish of Tongue will meet me and welcome me as the humble instrument of sending them to heaven.' I said, 'But have you not had seasons during your ministry when you could not speak with the same confidence?' 'Yes, frequently,' said he. 'I remember that on one occasion I had to preach for months with the rope about my neck, under the impression that all the religion I had was something I had learned from my pious mother. But all that is gone long ago – I know I shall be soon in my Father's house.'

There was no acute disease. He lingered on for days, and his state of mind was that of calm joy in the Lord. But on a Saturday morning his sun became clouded. Satan was suffered to tempt him; he looked on all his past religion as a delusion, and it was very painful to hear the sighs and groans of the venerable patriarch.

At four o'clock on Sabbath morning his son entered the room and the old man said, 'Hugh, I have good news for you. I was in such a state yesterday and last night that I could not pray for myself. But my dear people have evidently been earnest in prayer for me, for God has heard them and I have got the victory. That was but a cloud yesterday, a temptation. I have now no doubt of my interest in Christ, and I shall very soon see Him as He is.' In this state he continued till the evening, gradually sinking, and on the Lord's Day, the day he loved so well, he entered on his eternal rest.

Dr Angus Mackintosh

Dr Mackintosh was born in the parish of Moy in Inverness-shire.

He was the child of godly parents, and he told me an incident in his early history which made a lasting impression on him. When he was sixteen years old, his father assembled a few Christian friends, and after spending a part of the day in devotional exercises, he addressed his son as follows: 'When you were an infant, I cast you on God's covenant and took its seal for you. You have now come to years when you are able to think and act for yourself, and I now remind you that God's vows are on you; as a baptised person you have a special interest in the covenant, and that you are specially bound to give yourself to Christ, to receive Him as your own Saviour, and live to His glory.' Dr Mackintosh told me that the impression made on him that day was never wholly effaced.

Having resolved to study for the ministry he attended the university at King's College, Aberdeen.

Whilst there he enjoyed the friendship of Sir James Mackintosh and Robert Hall.

His first charge was the Gaelic Church in Glasgow, and at this early stage of it his ministry was eminently blessed. Mr Neil McBride, under whose ministry the awakening took place in Arran, was at that time his constant and earnest hearer.

After being four years in Glasgow he was translated to Tain in Ross-shire, and from that time till his death he was the great preacher of the north. There were at that time many eminent Christians in Ross and Sutherland, and they at once recognised in Mr Mackintosh the 'master in Israel.' After Hugh Mackenzie had heard him a few times, his minister, Mr Rainy, asked him what he thought of the young man who had come to Tain. His answer was: 'The great Ross-shire ministers, now gone, each had his own characteristic excellency. Mr MacPhail's preaching was experimental, Mr Fraser was the systematic divine, and Mr Porteous was the expounder of Scripture. And my belief is that Mr Mackintosh combines the excellencies of all the three.'

Let me attempt to describe him as I have seen him on a communion Sabbath at the tent. When it was known that he was to assist, thousands came from great distances, and it almost always happened that he presided on the Lord's Day, the tables being (of course) in the open air.[9]

He was a man six feet high, his dark brown eye was keen and piercing, and all his movements in the pulpit were beautifully graceful and suited to the subject. It was not art; it was nature. And yet you could not detect an awkward movement or what could be called a peculiarity.

He enters the tent and, after praise, he offers up a short, solemn, moving prayer. You feel that the man is speaking to God with the deepest reverence; every petition is like a bolt shot up to heaven. He reads his text and for a little time he is calm, with little action, and his deep-toned, melodious voice is, without the least effort on his part, heard by the most distant of eight or ten thousand people. He begins by expounding his text. His exposition is lucid and striking, and he shows you the great doctrines revealed in his text and the great lessons taught in it. He has thus laid a deep foundation for what is to follow. He has brought out the mind and will of God in the text – the whole addressed to the understanding – and now his application commences. His eye kindles and his voice, though not the least strained, is louder. Your attention is now thoroughly riveted. Your feeling is that the man

---

[9] The parish minister, in this case, took the English service, which was always in the church. [AM]

thoroughly believes what he says. His very countenance shows this. At one time you see deep, impressive compassion – a cloud on the countenance. At another time the sun breaks through the clouds and there is a beautiful smile.

The sermon is finished and he comes to the fencing[10] and, after a few solemn truths addressed to the worldly professor, he comes to deal with God's children, calling them to their Master's table. He speaks, indeed, to those of the highest attainments, showing that he knows their experience, but he is especially careful to deal tenderly with the 'bruised reed and the smoking flax'. He has great dramatic power. In his fine, pure Gaelic he puts questions and makes his hearers (so to speak) answer them, varying the tones of his voice as the subject varies. He follows the perplexed enquirer through all his wanderings; he comes down to the first breathings of the divine life in the soul, and he encourages the weakest to come, with all his darkness and perplexity, to meet Christ at His table. Experienced Christians, in comparing him with other ministers, were wont to say, 'No doubt they

---

[10] Before serving the Lord's Table, the minister solemnly 'fenced the table' by giving Scriptural marks of worthy and unworthy communicants. Fencing admonished intending communicants to search their consciences, so that unworthy participants would be deterred from going to the Lord's Table whereas worthy communicants would be invited. [RJD]

preach the gospel, and preach it powerfully, but Dr Mackintosh is the tender nurse – he knows how to *handle* the child.'

I recollect a striking example of this. He was to preach Gaelic on the Lord's Day at a communion in his neighbourhood. On Saturday, a very worthy man (but in this case, not very judicious man) preached a hard, scourging sermon from the words 'he that eateth and drinketh unworthily, eateth and drinketh judgment to himself.' There can be no doubt that he pushed the thing too far, for the feeling among good people, assembled from all quarters, was that if they were to be guided by what they had heard, they could not communicate next day. Dr Mackintosh presided on the Sabbath. He had not heard of the Saturday sermon. But if ever I saw the meekness and tenderness of Christ, I saw it on that day's fencing. And the result was, as many of the people told me, one of the most comfortable sacraments they had enjoyed for years. In fact, he had no sympathy with a system one sometimes met with – I mean the making a righteousness of keeping away from the communion table. I was present on one occasion when the communicants were rather stiff in coming to the table. He stood up in the tent and said, 'I never could reckon it an evidence of grace to be slow in coming to the Lord's Table. Whatever be the true believer's doubts and fears and discouragements, he will at once come with them all to the Lord's Table rather than displease or dishonour the Lord of the table.' It was like a shock of electricity – the table was filled in half a minute.

His table services were generally short. There was no *sermonising* in them; they were addressed directly to the communicants – or rather, to the individual believer – and their object always was to bring Christ and the believer face to face and (if I may so speak) to carry on the fellowship between them.

As the number of tables was often great, there was rarely an evening sermon; Dr Mackintosh generally concluded with an address. And it was here that he put forth his whole power and specially shone – these addresses were about the most striking things I ever listened to. After saying a few pithy words to the communicants as to their privileges and duties, he turned to the thousands of the young and thoughtless before him, and he spoke to them with a power and an unction and an authority which made the most careless listen. It was as if he said, 'I am God's servant and I have a message from God to you.'

In telling sinners of their danger, he spoke as one who saw it vividly. His fine eye was frequently filled with tears, and voice and manner made us feel as if thunder were rolling over our head. This was followed up by holding forth Christ as the living, present, all-gracious Saviour. And by the most melting appeals to the worst and the vilest to come to Him *even now*, with all their sins, that they might *even now* be saved. He seemed unwilling to part with them till they fled for refuge to Christ, and with a thorough knowledge of their own language and phrases, he plied them with illustrations and arguments.[11] He appeared to be realising the unseen world – indeed he said to me on one occasion that these were at times his happiest hours on earth. 'I have', said he, 'been frequently breathing the air of heaven whilst proclaiming to sinners Christ's fulness and love, and beseeching the worst of them to come to Him for salvation.'

His ministry was eminently blessed in his own parish, but in no part of his work did his Master more own him than he did in these addresses on communion Sabbaths. Giving me some directions at the commencement of my ministry, one of them was 'Never dismiss the people on the evening of a

---

[11] The ministers I knew in my younger days were thorough Calvinists, and they knew the system well, but they never allowed themselves to be hampered by their system in preaching Christ to sinners. You would not hear them qualifying and guarding and constantly putting in caveats, thus blunting the edge of the message. 'You are a lost sinner, Christ is here, He calls you to come to Him now, nothing can excuse disobedience.' Such was their preaching. [AM]

communion Sabbath without addressing the careless and godless, preaching Christ to them, and beseeching the chief of sinners to flee to Him for refuge. Their minds are then in a peculiar state, the scene they have witnessed has for the time softened and impressed them, and Christ's ambassador should take advantage of this.' And he then told me that for many years after he came to Ross-shire he had frequent opportunities of giving such addresses to immense congregations. Almost invariably after such seasons, persons from other parishes, sometimes as many as ten or twelve, came to consult him about their souls, and he generally found it was the evening address that made the impression.

About two years before his death he had a dangerous attack of illness, and he himself and others thought that it was the last messenger. I had the privilege of being constantly at his bedside, and the scene was unspeakably solemn and instructive.

An old friend and brother, Mr Forbes of Tarbat, came to see him, and I heard the following conversation pass between them. 'How are you, sir?' 'I am very weak – as weak as an infant.' 'I trust that though the outward man decayeth, the inward man is renewed day by day?' 'I have no doubt about that. I know whom I have believed, and am persuaded that He is able to keep that which I have committed to Him against that day.' Mr Forbes said with tears, and yet with a smile, 'There is many a poor Christian in Ross-shire would cheerfully take your sick bed to be able to speak as you do.' He answered with deep solemnity, 'I should now be the most miserable wretch on earth, unless I could speak as I have done.'

Whilst some of us were turning him in bed, he thanked us, and expressed regret for the trouble he was giving us, and then he said, 'My kind friends would, if they could, construct a bridge to take me over Jordan. But oh, with what contempt I can look at everything else, when I get but a glimpse of the finished work of Christ!'

After there was some hope of recovery, another old minister, a cousin of his own, said, 'I do trust God will still restore you to us in answer to the many prayers of His people.' And his answer was: 'I have no will in the matter. There have been seasons in my life when I had had a sinful impatience to die, and I have at other times had a sinful unwillingness to die, but He has enabled me now to put a blank bill into His hand. Here am I. Let Him do what seemeth Him good.'

God did restore him, and he preached again for about two years. He had promised to engage once more in the work he loved, to preach at a neighbouring sacrament, and to preach at the tent. But his work was done: before the time arrived, the hand of death had struck him, and amid sorrow deeper and more widespread than ever I saw in the north for any other death, the grave closed on Dr Angus Mackintosh.

Concluding remarks

I have endeavoured to describe a state of religion once to be met with in the North Highlands, but now to a large extent gone. There is still religion there – and I am persuaded, much real religion – but it presents to me a different aspect from what I once was acquainted with. With a few exceptions – 'two or three berries in the top of the uppermost bough' – there are not the glorious, enlightened, warm-hearted 'men' whom I knew in my younger days. There are not the Neil Mackenzies and the Donald Mathesons and the Angus Baillies and Andrew Rosses, any one of whom was a blessing in a parish, both to minister and people. But God has the residue of His Spirit. May He pour out His Spirit richly on His servants and people in these districts, and revive His own work in the midst of the years. 'Awake, awake, put on strength, O arm of the Lord; awake, as in the ancient days, in the generations of old.'

Printed in Great Britain
by Amazon